Written by
Carol Van Zanden

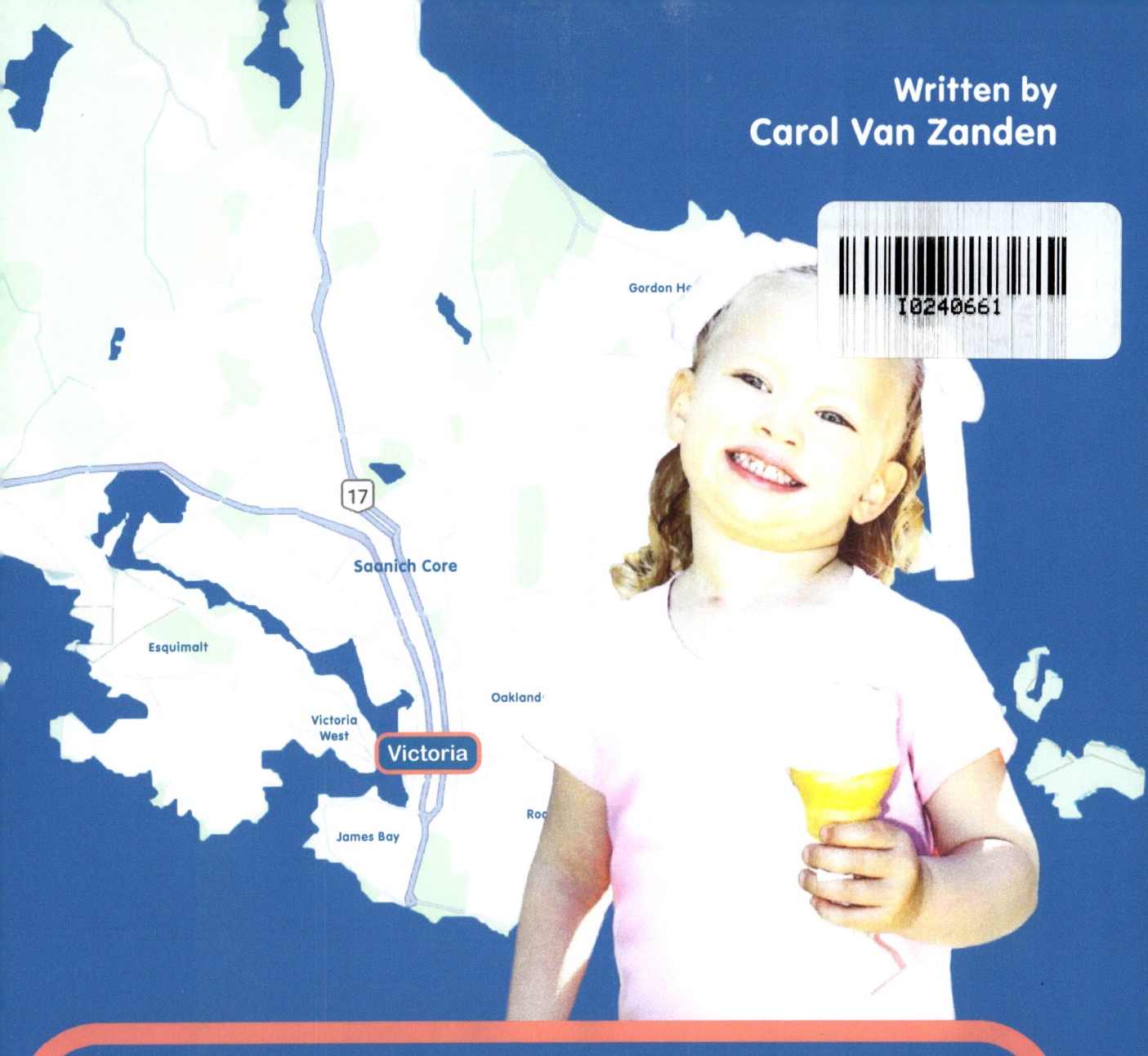

**TODAY IS SATURDAY...
TODAY IS SUNDAY...
TODAY IS MONDAY...**

I am on a ferry going to Victoria, B.C. with my family.

I can stand like the orca stands.

The statue grabs Bubba.
The man is not a statue!

This is called the Parliament Building.

It is lighted at night.

Today is Sunday.

It is Mother's Day. We are going to "High Tea" at the Empress Hotel. My family and I are riding in a coach.

This is the horse that pulls the coach.

**Bubba likes the horse.
So do I.**

This is the Empress Hotel.

This is Daddy's bowtie.

This is my brother Bubba at "High Tea."

This is me, Genevieve, at "High Tea."

This is my family at "High Tea" at the Empress Hotel.

We are in the garden at the
Empress Hotel.

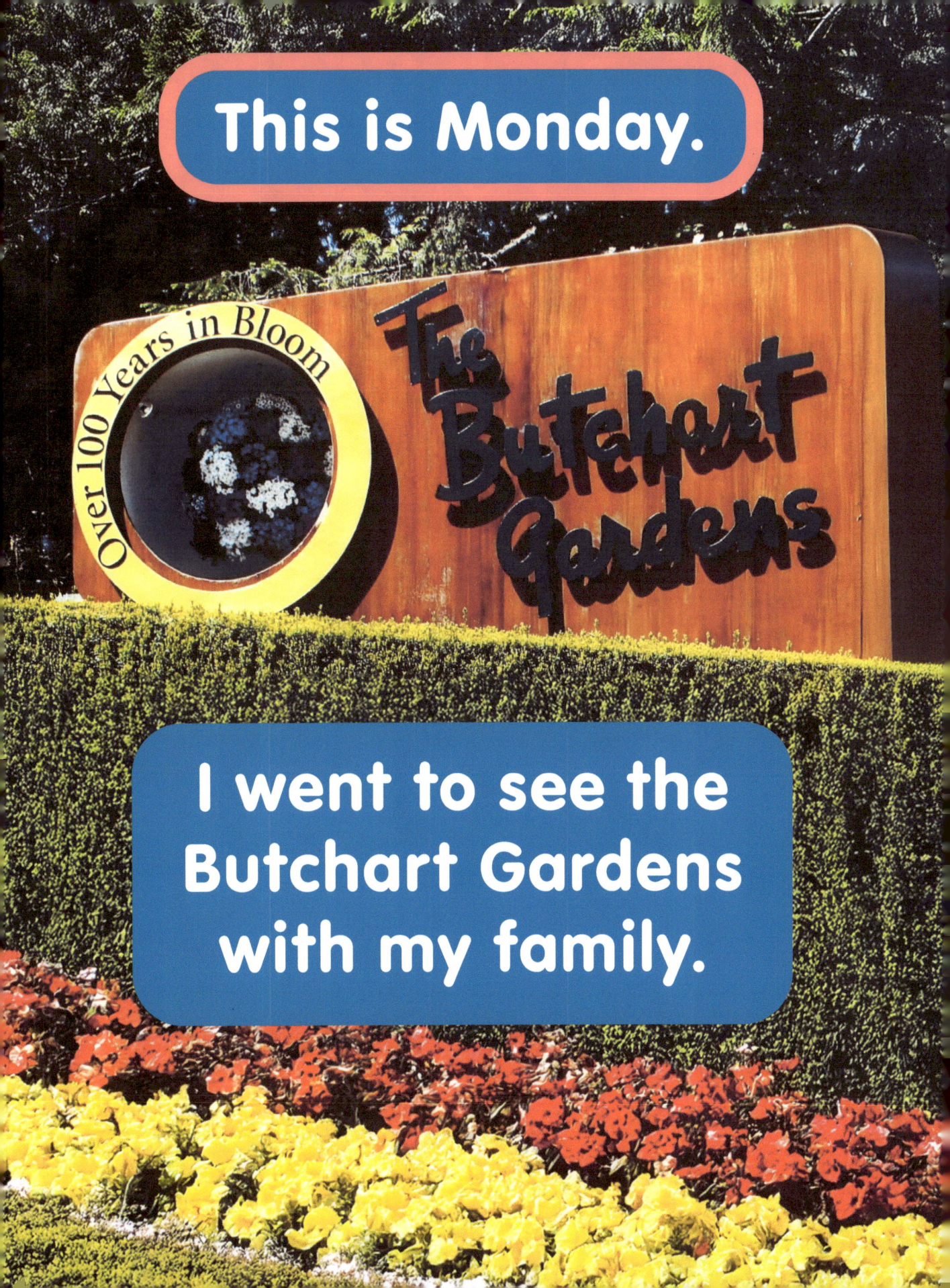

There is a merry-go-round at the Gardens.

Bubba likes the sunshine.

We all like the flowers.

It is time to go home.
Goodbye, little geyser.

Goodbye, Victoria, B.C.

Special Thanks

Genevieve and her family
for their contribution of family photos

popstradamus.com

Book design by Britt Sekulić

ISBN: 979-8-9916273-4-4

© 2024 Copyright Carol Van Zanden. All rights reserved.
MADE IN USA

About the Author

Carol Van Zanden is a retired Home Economics and kindergarten teacher who has lived in the Pacific Northwest all her life. With her BA and MA in Education, her professional career spanned over 38 years in early elementary, high school and as a college and adult educator. She and her husband, Ted, raised their children in Oak Harbor, Washington.

Through the years, Carol combined her love of family and photography, capturing memories of their grandchildren's visits with her camera. Years ago, she cut and pasted a series of books together using photos of her granddaughter and grandson to be read to by their parents and written in early childhood language for them to read by themselves. Not knowing that someday her prayers would be answered, with the help of self-publishing, and collaborating with a local bookmaker, the books would be brought to life professionally for other parents to read to their children and for them to read themselves.

Did you enjoy this book? Try other books in the series:

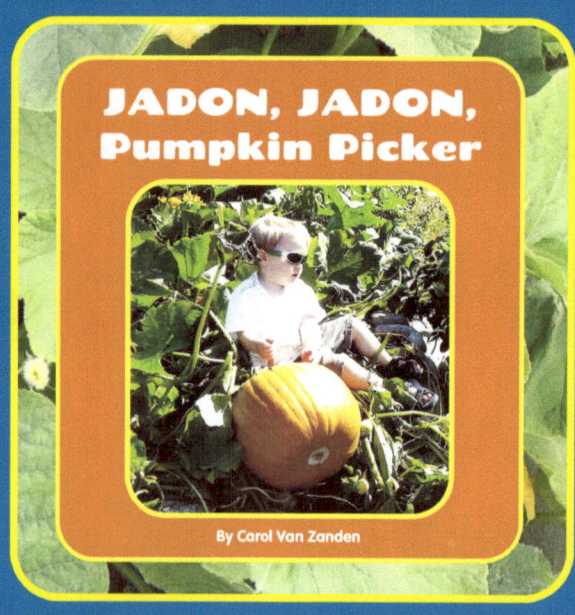

www.ingramcontent.com/pod-product-compliance
Lightning Source LLC
Chambersburg PA
CBHW061401090426
42743CB00002B/95